Growing Jesus' Way

Carolyn Nystrom

ILLUSTRATED BY EIRA REEVES

ISBN: 0–8024–7860–3

Designed and created by
Three's Company, 12 Flitcroft Street,
London WC2H 8DJ
Worldwide co-edition organized and
produced by Angus Hudson Ltd,
Concorde House, Grenville Place,
London NW7 3SA

Printed in Singapore

Moody Press, a ministry of the Moody
Bible Institute, is designed for
education, evangelization, and
edification. If we may assist you in
knowing more about Christ and the
Christian life, please write us without
obligation: Moody Press, c/o MLM,
Chicago, Illinois, 60610.

I grow.

Last summer I was forty-five inches tall, but this summer I measure forty-eight.

1

When Mom saw me in last year's pants, she laughed. "You grow so fast that I can hear you growing in the night." (I knew Mom was teasing.)

I change.

Last summer I liked my swings and sandbox best. But this summer I think riding a bike is more fun.

Last summer my job was to empty trash baskets, but this summer I'm learning to help in the garden.

That's all a part of growing.

3

Romans 10:9–10

I grow in other ways, too.
Last summer I became a Christian.
I said, "Jesus, I give You myself."

4

Romans 8:29; Galatians 2:20

Ever since then, I have been growing to be more and more like Jesus. Of course, I don't look like Him or dress like Him. Instead, I am learning to believe the things that Jesus taught and to do the things that Jesus did.

Jesus loves me so much that He has made me part of His family.

6

Philippians 2:14–16; 1 Corinthians 10:31

I love Jesus, too. I love Him so much that I want other people to know how wonderful He is. So I try to be as much like Jesus as I can. I want people to know what He is like by listening to what I say and watching what I do. They know that people in the same family often think alike.

But I can't always do right. And I don't always say the right things. God knows that, so He gives each Christian the Holy Spirit to live inside them. The Bible says that is like having "the mind of Christ."

Isaiah 61:10–11

I'm glad I don't have to make myself be good all alone.

9

And God gave me the Bible with stories about Jesus' life. Once when Jesus was teaching, some people brought a blind man to Him. Jesus took the blind man by the hand and led him away from the noisy crowd. Then Jesus put His hands on the man's eyes. When the man opened his eyes, he could see everything clearly.

Sally is a blind girl in my class at school. I can't make her see like Jesus could, but I can remember that lots of noise is confusing to Sally, so I explain to her what's going on. And when our class goes down the hall, I let her hold onto my arm so that she doesn't get lost.

That's Jesus' way.

11

Mark 6:30—44

Another time while Jesus was teaching, five thousand people came to listen. After listening to Jesus for a long time, the people were hungry. But they had not brought food with them, and there was no place near to buy food.

So Jesus took five loaves of bread and two fish. He broke them into small pieces and made enough food to feed all five thousand people until they were full.

I can't make enough food to feed five thousand people. But yesterday Pat forgot to bring her lunch to school. Some of the others said, "Too bad for you; you'll be hungry."

So at lunchtime, I sat next to Pat and gave her half of my lunch—even half of my chocolate cake. I was a little hungry after that, but that's all right.

It's Jesus' way.

Once when Jesus went to the Temple, He found people buying and selling animals. Jesus upset the tables of money and chased away the animals. He said, "What you are doing is not right. God's house is a place for all people to pray. You are making it a place to steal money."

14

I can help make things right, too. On the way home from school one day, I saw a crowd of big boys teasing a little boy. He had fallen into a mud puddle. The boys had taken away his toy dog and wouldn't give it back.

I was scared, but I yelled, "Stop that!" Then I elbowed my way in, grabbed the dog, helped the boy out of the mud, and marched off with him.

That's Jesus' way.

15

Mark 10:35—45

Once two of Jesus' disciples said, "We want to have the most important places in heaven." Then the other ten disciples got angry. Probably they thought, "Hey, we should be first."

So Jesus called them all together. He said, "No, you are all wrong. Other people try to get the best place for themselves, but My people are different. We must take care of each other."

16

I think of that when we are in line for ice cream. Nobody likes to be at the back of the line. But I try not to complain if the others push to the front.

That's Jesus' way.

Satan came to Jesus and tempted Him to do wrong. Satan said, "I will give you the whole world if only you will bow down and worship me."

Jesus must have wanted the whole world to belong to Him. But He said no to Satan.

I want things, too. More than anything, I want a blue brooch. I saw one once in my cousin's room. I could have put it in my pocket and walked away. *No one will ever know,* I thought.

But I know that stealing is wrong. So I put my hand in my pocket instead, and I left the room.

That's Jesus' way.

19

One of Jesus' friends asked, "If my brother does something mean to me, how many times should I forgive him?"

Jesus answered, "Forgive him—even if he does the same things seven times in one day."

Later, when Jesus died, He prayed for the men who were killing Him. He said, "Father, forgive them; they don't know what they are doing."

20

To be like Jesus, I must forgive people, too. Last week, my sister broke my favorite necklace. She said, "I'm sorry, Cathy."

I felt bad about my necklace. But I said, "That's all right, Ruth." And I hugged her.

That's Jesus' way.

Jesus believed that prayer is important. When He was busy teaching all day, He got up early in the morning, while it was still dark, so He would have time alone to talk with God, His Father.

22

If it was important for Jesus to pray, it is important for me, too. I can talk to God about anything, anytime, anywhere. But each day I should take some time to talk to God.

It's Jesus' way.

23

Because I belong to Jesus, I am different from people who are not in His family. When other people are deciding what to do, they usually ask themselves, "What is best for me?"

But a Christian will ask, "What would please Jesus?"

24

1 Corinthians 6:11; Leviticus 20:26

So those who choose Jesus' way will sometimes have to separate from other people.

My friends chose to go to a store after school and steal candy bars. They asked me to come too. But I played in the park instead. We went different ways.

Hebrews 13:20–21; 2 Peter 1:3–4

It's hard to be different, but God gives me lots of help. The Holy Spirit lives inside me. He reminds me to pray to Him and ask Him for help. Then He gives me just what I need.

God gives me the Bible. There He tells me exactly what is right and wrong—so I don't have to guess.

And God gives me the church with lots of other Christians. We can help each other live the way God wants us to.

27

1 John 1:8—2:2

Even with all that help, I will still sometimes do wrong. God knows that, so He says in the Bible, "Tell Me you are sorry, and I will forgive you."

Romans 8:38–39

God still loves me when I do wrong. And God will keep on loving me forever.

1 John 3:1—2

Ever so slowly God is helping me to grow more and more like Jesus. I'm not finished yet, but when I see Jesus in heaven, I'll be just like Him: perfect.